PENGUIN BOOKS

LETTER TO A PRIEST

Philosopher, political activist, social critic, and mystic, Simone Weil was one of the most original and rigorous thinkers of the twentieth century. Born into an upper class family in Paris in 1909, Weil spent much of her life performing manual labor in factories and fields in order to understand the needs of workers and fought briefly in the Spanish Revolution. Hailed by T. S. Eliot as "a woman of genius, a kind of genius akin to that of the saints," Weil's work displays striking insight on issues of class, politics, and religion. Her sixteen volumes of posthumously published works include *Gravity and Grace* (1963) and *The Need for Roots* (1952). She died in 1943, at the age of thirty-four, while working as an advocate for the Free French movement.

LETTER
TO A PRIEST

---

by
SIMONE WEIL

PENGUIN BOOKS

PENGUIN BOOKS

Published by the Penguin Group
Penguin Putnam Inc., 375 Hudson Street,
New York, New York 10014, U.S.A.
Penguin Books Ltd, 80 Strand, London WC2R 0RL, England
Penguin Books Australia Ltd, 250 Camberwell Road,
Camberwell, Victoria 3124, Australia
Penguin Books Canada Ltd, 10 Alcorn Avenue,
Toronto, Ontario, Canada M4V 3B2
Penguin Books India (P) Ltd, 11 Community Centre,
Panchsheel Park, New Delhi – 110 017, India
Penguin Books (N.Z.) Ltd, Cnr Rosedale and Airborne Roads,
Albany, Auckland, New Zealand
Penguin Books (South Africa) (Pty) Ltd, 24 Sturdee Avenue,
Rosebank, Johannesburg 2196, South Africa

Penguin Books Ltd, Registered Offices:
Harmondsworth, Middlesex, England

First published in France as *Lettre à un religieux* 1951
First published in the United States of America by G. P. Putnam's Sons 1954
Published in Penguin Books 2003

1   3   5   7   9   10   8   6   4   2

LIBRARY OF CONGRESS CATALOGING IN PUBLICATION DATA
Weil, Simone, 1909–1943.
[Lettre à un religieux. English]
Letter to a Priest / by Simone Weil.
p.   cm.
ISBN 0 14 20.0267 4
1. Catholic Church—Controversial literature.   I. Title.
B2430.W4373 L413 2003
282—dc21   2002034603

Printed in the United States of America

NOTE

This letter was addressed by Simone Weil to a French priest living in New York when she was staying there in the autumn of 1942, waiting to join the Free French Movement in London.

LETTER
TO A PRIEST

WHEN I read the catechism of the Council of Trent, it seems as though I had nothing in common with the religion there set forth. When I read the New Testament, the mystics, the liturgy, when I watch the celebration of the mass, I feel with a sort of conviction that this faith is mine or, to be more precise, would be mine without the distance placed between it and me by my imperfection. This results in a painful spiritual state. I would like to make it, not less painful, only clearer. Any pain whatsoever is acceptable where there is clarity.

I am going to enumerate for you a certain number of thoughts which have dwelt in me for years (some of them at least) and which form a barrier between me and the Church. I do not ask you to discuss their basis. I should be happy for there to be such a discussion, but later on, in the second place.

9

I ask you to give me a definite answer—leaving out such expressions as 'I think that', etc.—regarding the compatibility or incompatibility of each of these opinions with membership of the Church. If there is any incompatibility, I should like you to say straight out: I would refuse baptism (or absolution) to anybody claiming to hold the opinions expressed under the headings numbered so-and-so, so-and-so and so-and-so. I do not ask for a quick answer. There is no hurry. All I ask for is a categorical answer.

I must apologize for giving you this trouble, but I do not see how I can avoid it. I am far from regarding meditation on these problems as a game. Not only is it of more than vital importance, seeing that one's eternal salvation is at stake; but, furthermore, it is of an importance which far surpasses in my opinion that of my own salvation. A problem of life and death is a game by comparison.

Among the opinions that are to follow there are some about which I am doubtful; but were it a strict article of the faith to esteem them false, I should regard them as being as serious an obstacle as the others, for I am firmly convinced that they are held in doubt by me, that is to say, that it is not legitimate to deny them categorically.

Some of these opinions (more particularly those which concern the Mysteries, the Scriptures not of Jewish-Christian inspiration, Melchisedec, etc.) have never been condemned, although it is very likely that they were upheld in the early centuries. This makes me wonder if they were not secretly accepted. However that may be, if today they were to be publicly proclaimed by me or by others and condemned by the Church, I would not abandon them, unless it could be proved to me that they were false.

I have been thinking about these things for years with all the intensity of love and attention of which I am capable. This intensity is a wretchedly feeble one because of my imperfection which is very great; but it seems to me it is always on the increase. In proportion as it grows, the bonds which attach me to the Catholic faith become ever stronger and stronger, ever more deeply rooted in the heart and intelligence. But at the same time the thoughts which separate me from the Church also gain in force and clarity. If these thoughts are really incompatible with membership of the Church, then there is no hope that I may ever take part in the sacraments. If such is the case, I do not see how I can avoid the conclusion that my vocation is to be a Christian outside the Church. The possibility of there being such a vocation would imply that the Church is not Catholic in fact as it is in name, and that it must one day become so, if it is destined to fulfil its mission.

The opinions which follow have for me various degrees of probability or certainty, but all go accompanied in my mind by a question-mark. If I express them in the indicative mood it is only because of the poverty of language; my needs would require that the conjugation should contain a supplementary tense. In the domain of holy things I affirm nothing categorically. But such of my opinions as are in conformity with the teaching of the Church also go accompanied in my mind by the same question-mark.

I look upon a certain suspension of judgment with regard to all thoughts whatever they may be, without any exception, as constituting the virtue of humility in the domain of the intelligence.

Here is the list:

I

If we take a moment in history anterior to Christ and sufficiently remote from him—for example, five centuries before his time—and we set aside what follows afterwards, at that moment Israel has less of a share in God and in divine truth than several of the surrounding peoples (India, Egypt, Greece, China). For the essential truth concerning God is that He is good. To believe that God can order men to commit atrocious acts of injustice and cruelty is the greatest mistake it is possible to make with regard to Him.

Zeus, in the *Iliad*, orders no cruelty whatever. The Greeks believed that 'suppliant Zeus' inhabits every miserable creature that implores pity. Jehovah is the 'God of hosts'. The history of the Hebrews shows that this refers not only to the stars, but also to the warriors of Israel. Now, Herodotus enumerates a great number of Hellenic and Asiatic peoples amongst whom there was *only one* that had a 'Zeus of hosts'. This blasphemy was unknown to all the others. The Egyptian *Book of the Dead*, at least three thousand years old, and doubtless very much older, is filled with evangelic charity. (The dead man says to Osiris: 'Lord of Truth, I bring thee the truth . . . I have destroyed evil for thee . . . I have killed no man. I have made no man weep. I have let no man suffer hunger. I have never been the cause of a master's doing harm to his slave. I have never made any man afraid. I have never adopted a haughty tone. I have never turned a deaf ear to just and true words. I have never put my name forward for honours. I have not spurned God in His manifestations. . . .')

The Hebrews, who for four centuries were in contact with Egyptian civilization, refused to adopt this sweet spirit. They wanted power. . . .

All the texts dating from before the exile are, I think, tainted with this fundamental error concerning God—except the Book of Job, the hero of which is not a Jew, the Song of Solomon (but does it date from before the exile?) and certain psalms of David (but have they been correctly attributed?). Otherwise, the first absolutely pure character appearing in Jewish history is Daniel (who was initiated into Chaldean lore). The lives of all the others, beginning with Abraham, are sullied by atrocious things. (Abraham starts off by prostituting his wife.)

This would incline one to think that Israel learnt the most essential truth about God (namely, that God is good before being powerful) from foreign traditional sources, Chaldean, Persian or Greek, and thanks to the exile.

2

What we call idolatry is to a large extent an invention of Jewish fanaticism. All peoples at all times have always been monotheistic. If some Hebrews of classical Jewry were to return to life and were to be provided with arms, they would exterminate the lot of us—men, women and children, for the crime of idolatry. They would reproach us for worshipping Baal and Astarte, taking Christ for Baal and the Virgin for Astarte.

Conversely, Baal and Astarte were perhaps representations of Christ and the Virgin.

Some of these cults have been justly accused of the debauches that accompanied them—but, I think, far less often than it is supposed today.

But the cruelties bound up with the cult of Jehovah, the exterminations commanded by him, are defilements at least as atrocious. Cruelty is a still more appalling crime than lust. Moreover, lust satisfies itself as readily by murder as it does by sexual intercourse.

The feelings of the so-called pagans for their statues were very probably the same as those inspired nowadays by the crucifix and the statues of the Virgin, with the same deviations among people of mediocre spiritual and intellectual development.

Is not such-and-such a supernatural virtue commonly attributed to some particular statue of the Virgin?

Even if they did happen to believe the divinity to be totally present in some stone or wood, it may be they were sometimes right. Do we not believe God is present in some bread and wine? Perhaps God was actually present in statues fashioned and consecrated according to certain rites.

The veritable idolatry is covetousness (πλεονεξία, ἥτις ἐστίν εἰδωλολατρεία, Col. iii. 5), and the Jewish nation, in its thirst for carnal good, was guilty of this in the very moments even when it was worshipping its God. The Hebrews took for their idol, not something made of metal or wood, but a race, a nation, something just as earthly. Their religion is essentially inseparable from such idolatry, because of the notion of the 'chosen people'.

3

The ceremonies of the Eleusinian mysteries and of those of Osiris were regarded as sacraments in the sense in which we understand that term today. And *it may be* they were real sacraments, possessing the same virtue as baptism or the eucharist, and deriving that virtue from the same relation with Christ's Passion. The Passion was then to come. Today it is past. Past and future are symmetrical.

Chronology cannot play a decisive role in a relationship between God and man, a relationship one of the terms of which is eternal.

If the Redemption, with the sensible signs and means corresponding to it, had not been present on this earth from the very beginning, it would not be possible to pardon God—if one may use such words without blasphemy—for the affliction of so many innocent people, so many people uprooted, enslaved, tortured and put to death in the course of centuries preceding the Christian era. Christ is present on this earth, unless men drive him away, wherever there is crime and affliction. Without the supernatural effects of this presence, how would the innocent, crushed beneath the weight of affliction, be able to avoid falling into the crime of cursing God, and consequently into damnation?

Moreover, St. John talks about the 'Lamb slain from the foundation of the world'.

The proof that the content of Christianity existed before Christ is that since his day there have been no very noticeable changes in men's behaviour.

4

There have *perhaps* been among various peoples (India, Egypt, China, Greece) sacred Scriptures revealed in the same manner as the Jewish-Christian Scriptures. Some of the texts which still exist today are possibly either fragments or echoes of them.

5

The passages in the Bible (Genesis, Psalms, St. Paul) concerning Melchisedec prove that from the dawn of Israel there existed outside Israel a service of and knowledge of God situated on the selfsame level as Christianity and infinitely superior to anything Israel itself has ever possessed.

There is nothing to exclude the supposition of a link between Melchisedec and the ancient mysteries. There is an affinity between bread and Demeter, wine and Dionysus.

Melchisedec is apparently, according to Genesis, a king of Canaan. Hence, in all probability, the corruption and impiety of the villages of Canaan either dated back only a few centuries at the time of the massacres, or else were libellous inventions levelled against their victims by the Hebrews.

6

The passage in St. Paul concerning Melchisedec, taken in connection with Christ's words 'Abraham hath seen my day', might even indicate that Melchisedec was already an Incarnation of the Word.

At all events, we do not know for certain that there have not been incarnations previous to that of Jesus, and that Osiris in Egypt, Krishna in India were not of that number.

7

If Osiris is not a man having lived on earth while remaining God, in the same way as Christ, then at any rate the story of Osiris is a prophecy infinitely clearer, more complete and closer to the truth than everything which goes by that name in the Old Testament. The same applies to other gods that have died and returned to life.

The extreme importance *at the present day* of this problem comes from the fact that it is becoming a matter of urgency to remedy the divorce which has existed for twenty centuries and goes on getting worse and worse between profane civilization and spirituality in Christian countries. Our civilization owes nothing to Israel and very little to Christianity; it owes nearly everything to pre-Christian antiquity (Germans, Druids, Rome, Greece, Aegeo-Cretans, Phoenicians, Egyptians, Babylonians . . .). If there is a watertight division between this antiquity and Christianity, the same water-tight division exists between our profane life and our spiritual life. For Christianity to become truly incarnated, for the whole of life to become permeated by the Christian inspiration, it must first of all be recognized that, historically, our profane civilization is derived from a religious inspiration which, although chronologically pre-Christian, was Christian in essence. God's widsom must be regarded as the unique source of all light upon earth, even such feeble lights as those which illumine the things of this world.

And the same applies in the case of Prometheus. The story of Prometheus is the very story of Christ projected into the eternal. All that is wanting is its localization in time and space.

Greek mythology is full of prophecies; so are the stories drawn from European folklore, what are known as fairy tales.

Many of the names of Greek divinities are probably in reality various names for designating one single divine Person, namely the Word. I think this is so in the case of Dionysus, Apollo, Artemis, celestial Aphrodite, Prometheus, Eros, Proserpina and several others.

I also think that Hestia, Athene and possibly Hephaestus are names for the Holy Spirit. Hestia is the central Fire. Athene came forth from the head of Zeus after the latter had devoured his wife, Wisdom, who was pregnant; she 'proceeds', therefore, from God and his Wisdom. Her emblem is the olive, and oil, in the Christian sacraments, is symbolically connected with the Holy Spirit.

Certain actions performed by Christ, certain words of his are constantly commented upon as follows: 'The prophecies must needs be fulfilled.' This refers to the Hebrew prophecies. But there are other actions, other words which might be commented upon in the same way in connection with the non-Hebrew prophecies.

Christ began his public life by changing the water into wine. He ended it by transforming the wine into blood. He thus marked his affinity to Dionysus. And again by the words: 'I am the true vine'.

The words: 'Except a corn of wheat die' express his affinity to the dead and resuscitated divinities which were represented by vegetation, such as Attis and Proserpina.

The motherhood of the Virgin has mysterious connections with some words in Plato's *Timaeus* concerning a certain essence, mother of all things and for ever intact. All the mother Goddesses of antiquity, like Demeter, Isis, were figures of the Virgin.

The comparison again and again insisted upon between the Cross and a tree, between the crucifixion and a hanging, must be connected with mythologies that have now disappeared.

If the date of the Scandinavian poem the *Rune of Odin* is prior to any possible Christian influence (which is unverifiable), it also contains a very striking prophecy:

'I know that I hung on a wind-swept tree for nine full nights, pierced with a spear and offered up to Odin, I to myself; on the tree whereof no man can tell what are the roots from which it springs.

'None gave me bread, or a horn to drink from. I looked down, I applied myself to the runes, weeping I learnt them, then I came down from there.' (First Edda.)

The term 'Lamb of God' is no doubt connected with traditions having possibly links with what is nowadays called totemism. The story of Zeus Ammon in Herodotus (Zeus slaying a ram in order to appear, covered with its fleece, before the person who entreats him to allow himself to be seen), considered in connection with the words of St. John: 'The Lamb slain from the foundation of the world', throws a penetrating light on this subject. The first sacrifice that was pleasing to God, that of Abel, recalled in the canon of the mass as an image of that of Christ, was an animal sacrifice. The same applies in the case of the second one, Noah's, which definitively saved humanity from the wrath of God and brought about a pact between God and mankind. These are precisely the effects of Christ's Passion. There is a very mysterious relationship between the two.

People must have thought in very ancient times that God is actually present in animals killed to be eaten; that God in fact descends into them for the purpose of offering himself as food to man. This notion turned animal food into a communion, whereas otherwise it is a crime, unless we adopt a more or less Cartesian philosophy.*

Perhaps at Thebes, in Egypt, God was actually present in the ram sacrificed ritually, as He is today in the consecrated host.

It is worth noticing that at the moment Christ was crucified, the sun was in the constellation of the Ram.

Plato, in *Timaeus*, describes the astronomical constitution of the universe as a sort of crucifixion of the Soul of the World, the point of intersection being the equinoctial point, that is to say, the constellation of the Ram.

* Old Testament

Several texts (*Epinomis*, *Timaeus*, *Symposium*, Philolaos, Proclus) indicate that the geometrical construction of the proportional mean between a number and unity—the central fact in Greek geometry—was the symbol of the divine mediation between God and man.

Now, a considerable number of Christ's sayings reported in the Gospels (especially St. John) have with a very marked insistence, which can only have been designed intentionally, the algebraical form of the proportional mean. For example: 'As my Father hath sent me, even so send I you, etc.' A single relationship unites the Father to Christ, Christ to his disciples. Christ is the proportional mean between God and the Saints. The very word mediation indicates this.

From this I conclude that just as Christ recognized himself in the Messiah of the Psalms, the Just One who suffers in Isaiah, the bronze serpent of Genesis, so in the same way he recognized himself in the proportional mean of Greek geometry, which thus becomes the most resplendent of the prophecies.

Ennius, in a Pythagorean writing, says: 'The moon is called Proserpina . . . because, *like a serpent*, she is twisted now towards the left now towards the right.'

All the mediatory gods that may be likened to the Word are lunar gods, wearers of horns, lyres or bows representing the crescent moon (Osiris, Artemis, Apollo, Hermes, Dionysus, Zagreus, Eros . . .). Prometheus forms an exception, but in Aeschylus Io stands for his counterpart, condemned to perpetual vagabondage as he is to crucifixion—and she is horned. (It is worth remembering that before he was crucified Christ was a vagabond—and Plato depicts Eros as a wretched vagabond.)

If the Sun is the image of the Father, the Moon, perfect reflection of solar splendour, but a reflection we can gaze upon and which suffers diminution and disappearance, is the image of the Son. The light is then that of the Spirit.

Heraclitus recognized a Trinity, which we can only divine from the fragments of his that remain to us, but which stands out clearly in the Hymn to Zeus of Cleanthus of Heraclitian inspiration. The Persons are: Zeus, the Logos and the divine Fire or Lightning.

Cleanthus says to Zeus: 'This universe *consents* to thy domination (ἑκὼν κρατεῖται)—Such is the virtue of the servitor that thou holdest under thine invincible hands—Flaming, two-edged, eternally living, the lightning.' The lightning is not an instrument of coercion, but a fire which arouses voluntary consent and obedience. It is therefore Love. And this Love is a servitor, an eternally living presence, hence a Person. Those very ancient representations of Zeus with a two-edged axe (symbol of lightning) on Cretan bas-reliefs already possessed perhaps this significance. We may draw the parallel between 'two-edged' and Christ's words: 'I am not come to bring peace, but a sword.'

Fire is constantly the symbol of the Holy Spirit in the New Testament.

The Stoics, heirs of Heraclitus, named *pneuma* the fire whose energy sustains the order of the world. *Pneuma*, that is fiery breath.

The semen which produces carnal generation was, according to them and according to the Pythagoreans, a *pneuma* mixed with liquid.

Christ's words about being born anew—and consequently the whole symbolism of baptism— must so as to be properly understood be considered more particularly in relation to the Pythagorean and Stoic conceptions concerning generation. Justin, moreover, I think, compares baptism to generation. Hence the Orphic words: 'Kid, thou art fallen into milk' must perhaps be understood in connection with baptism (the Ancients looked upon milk as being composed of the father's seminal fluid).

The celebrated expression 'Great Pan is dead' was perhaps meant to announce, not the disappearance of idolatry, but the death of Christ—Christ being the Great Pan, the great All. Plato (*Cratylus*) says that Pan is the 'logos'. In *Timaeus* he gives this name to the Soul of the World.

St. John in making use of the words Logos and Pneuma, indicated the profound relationship existing between Greek Stoicism (to be distinguished from that of Cato and Brutus!) and Christianity.

Plato also clearly recognized and by allusions in his works pointed to the dogmas of the Trinity, Mediation, the Incarnation, the Passion, and to the notions of grace and salvation through love. He recognized the essential truth, namely, that God is the Good. He is only the All-powerful by way of addition.

In saying: 'I am come to send fire on the earth; and what will I, if it be already kindled?', Christ indicated his kinship with Prometheus.

His words: 'I am the Way' should be compared with the Chinese 'Tao', a word signifying literally 'the way' and metaphorically, on the one hand the method of salvation, and on the other hand the impersonal God who is the God of Chinese spirituality, but who, although impersonal, is the model for the wise and acts continually.

His words: 'I am the Truth' call to mind Osiris, Lord of Truth.

When in one of his most important teachings he says: 'They which do the truth' (ηοιοῦντες ἀλήθειαν), he uses an expression which is not a Greek one, and which, as far as I know, is not a Hebrew one (must verify this). On the other hand, it is an Egyptian one. *Maât* means at the same time justice and truth. That is significant. No doubt it is not for nothing that the Holy Family went down into Egypt.

Baptism regarded as a death is the equivalent of the ancient initiations. St. Clement Roman uses the word 'initiated' in the sense of baptized. The use of the word 'mysteries' to designate the sacraments points to the same equivalence. The circular font strongly resembles the stone basin in which, according to Herodotus, the mystery of Osiris's passion was celebrated. They both represent perhaps the open sea, that open sea on which floated Noah's ark and that of Osiris, wooden structures which saved humanity before the one of the Cross.

Any number of accounts drawn from mythology and folklore could be translated into Christian truths without forcing or deforming anything in them, but rather, on the contrary, thus throwing a vivid light upon them. And these truths, would in their turn, thereby take on a new clarity.

8

Every time that a man has, with a pure heart, called upon Osiris, Dionysus, Krishna, Buddha, the Tao, etc., the Son of God has answered him by sending the Holy Spirit. And the Holy Spirit has acted upon his soul, not by inciting him to abandon his religious tradition, but by bestowing upon him light—and in the best of cases the fulness of light —in the heart of that same religious tradition.

Prayer with the Greeks bore a strong resemblance to Christian prayer. When Aeschylus says, in the *Frogs* of Aristophanes: 'Demeter, thou who hast nourished my thoughts, may I be worthy of thy mysteries!', that strongly resembles a prayer to the Virgin, and must have had the same virtue. Aeschylus gives a perfect description of contemplation in the magnificent lines: 'Whosoever, his thoughts turned toward Zeus, shall proclaim his glory, the same shall receive the fulness of wisdom.' (He recognized the Trinity: ' . . . by the side of Zeus there stand his act and his word'.)

It is, therefore, useless to send out missions to prevail upon the peoples of Asia, Africa or Oceania to enter the Church.

9

When Christ said: 'Go ye therefore, and teach all nations, and bring them the glad tidings', he commanded his apostles to bring glad tidings, not a theology. He himself, having come, as he said, 'only for the sheep of the house of Israel', added these good tidings on to the religion of Israel.

He probably wished that each of the apostles should in the same way add the good tidings of the life and death of Christ on to the religion of the country in which he happened to find himself. But the command was misunderstood, because of the ineradicable nationalism of the Jews. They must needs impose their Scriptures everywhere.

If it is thought that it shows a lot of presumption to suppose that the apostles misunderstood Christ's commands, I can only answer that there is no doubt at all that they did display incomprehension with regard to certain points. For after Christ had risen and had said: Go and teach the nations (or the Gentiles) and baptize them; after He had spent forty days with his disciples revealing his doctrine to them, Peter had to have, nevertheless, a special revelation and a dream before being able to make up his mind to baptize a heathen; he found it necessary to invoke this dream in order to explain this action to his followers; and Paul had great difficulty in eliminating circumcision.

Besides, it is written that the tree shall be known by its fruits. The Church has borne too many evil fruits for there not to have been some mistake made at the beginning.

Europe has been spiritually uprooted, cut off from that antiquity in which all the elements of our civilization have their origin; and she has gone about uprooting the other continents from the sixteenth century onwards.

After twenty centuries, Christianity has, practically speaking, not penetrated outside the white race; Catholicism is much more limited still in extent. America remained for sixteen centuries without hearing Christ spoken of (yet St. Paul had said: Glad Tidings which have been announced to the *whole* of creation) and the nations living there were destroyed in the midst of the most appalling cruelties before ever having had the time to know Him. Missionary zeal has not Christianized Africa, Asia and Oceania, but has brought these territories under the cold, cruel and destructive domination of the white race, which has trodden down everything.

It would be strange, indeed, that the word of Christ should have produced such results if it had been properly understood.

Christ said: 'Go ye, and teach all nations and baptize those who believe', that is to say, those who believe on Him. He never said: 'Compel them to renounce all that their ancestors have looked upon as sacred, and to adopt as a holy book the history of a small nation unknown to them.' I have been assured that the Hindus would in no way be prevented by their own tradition from receiving baptism, were it not for the fact that the missionaries make it a condition that they must renounce Vishnu and Shiva. If a Hindu believes that Vishnu is the Word and Shiva the Holy Spirit, and that the Word was incarnate in Krishna and in Rama before being so in Jesus, by what right can he be refused baptism? In the same way, in the quarrel between the Jesuits and the Papacy over the missions in China, it was the Jesuits who were carrying out the words of Christ.

10

Missionary action in the way in which it is, in fact, conducted (especially since the condemnation of Jesuit policy in China in the seventeenth century) is bad, save perhaps in certain individual cases. The missionaries—even the martyrs amongst them—are too closely accompanied by guns and battleships for them to be true witnesses of the Lamb. I have never heard that the Church has ever officially condemned punitive expeditions undertaken to avenge the missionaries.

Personally, I should never give even as much as a sixpence towards any missionary enterprise. I think that for any man a change of religion is as dangerous a thing as a change of language is for a writer. It may turn out a success, but it can also have disastrous consequences.

II

The Catholic religion contains explicitly truths which other religions contain implicitly. But, conversely, other religions contain explicitly truths which are only implicit in Christianity. The most well-informed Christian can still learn a great deal concerning divine matters from other religious traditions; although inward spiritual light can also cause him to apprehend everything through the medium of his own tradition. All the same, were these other traditions to disappear from the face of the earth, it would be an irreparable loss. The missionaries have already made far too many of them disappear as it is.

St. John of the Cross compares faith to reflections of silver, truth being gold. The various authentic religious traditions are different reflections of the same truth, and perhaps equally precious. But we do not realize this, because each of us lives only one of these traditions and sees the others from the outside. But, as Catholics are for ever repeating—and rightly—to unbelievers, a religion can only be known from the inside.

It is as if two men, installed in two communicating rooms, each one seeing the sun through the window and his neighbour's wall lit up by the rays, each thought that he alone saw the sun and that all his neighbour had was its reflection.

The Church recognizes that vocational diversity is a precious thing. This conception needs to be extended to vocations that are outside the Church. For there are some.

12

As the Hindus say, God is at the same time personal and impersonal. He is impersonal in the sense that his infinitely mysterious manner of being a Person is infinitely different from the human manner. It is only possible to grasp this mystery by employing at the same time, like two pincers, these two contrary notions, incompatible here on earth, compatible only in God. (The same applies to many other pairs of contraries, as the Pythagoreans had realized.)

One is able to think of God at the same time, not successively, as being three and one (a thing which few Catholics manage to be able to do) only by thinking of Him at the same time as personal and impersonal. Otherwise one represents Him to oneself sometimes as a single divine Person, at other times as three Gods. Many Christians confuse such an oscillation with true faith.

Saints of a very lofty spirituality, like St. John of the Cross, have seized simultaneously and with an equal force both the personal and the impersonal aspects of God. Less developed souls concentrate their attention and their faith above all or exclusively upon one or other of these two aspects. Thus little St. Theresa of Lisieux only represented to herself a personal God.

As in the West the word God, taken in its usual meaning, signifies a Person, men whose attention, faith and love are almost exclusively concentrated on the impersonal aspect of God can actually believe themselves and declare themselves to be atheists, even though supernatural love inhabits their souls. Such men are surely saved.

They can be recognized by their attitude with regard to the things of this world. All those who possess in its pure state the love of their neighbour and the acceptance of the order of the world, including affliction—all those, even should they live and die to all appearances atheists, are surely saved.

Those who possess perfectly these two virtues, even should they live and die atheists, are saints.

When one comes across such men, it is futile to want to convert them. They are wholly converted, though not visibly so; they have been begotten anew by water and the spirit, even if they have never been baptized; they have eaten of the bread of life, even if they have never communicated.

13

Charity and faith, though distinct, are inseparable. The two forms of charity still more so. Whoever is capable of a movement of pure compassion towards a person in affliction (a very rare thing anyway) possesses, maybe implicitly, yet always really, the love of God and faith.

Christ does not save all those who say to Him:

'Lord, Lord.' But he saves all those who out of a pure heart give a piece of bread to a starving man, without thinking about Him the least little bit. And these, when He thanks them, reply: 'Lord, when did we feed thee?'

Hence St. Thomas's affirmation, that he who refuses his assent to a single article of faith does not possess the faith in any degree, is false, unless it can be established that heretics have never possessed charity towards their neighbour. But that would be difficult to do. As far as we are able to tell, the 'perfect ones' among the Cathari, for example, possessed it to a degree very rarely found even among the saints.

If one were to make out that the devil contrives the appearance of such virtues in heretics in order the better to seduce souls, it would be going against the words: 'Ye shall know the tree by its fruits'; it would be arguing exactly like those who re-garded Christ as possessed of a devil, and perhaps coming very close to committing the unpardonable sin, blasphemy against the Holy Spirit.

So likewise an atheist or an 'infidel', capable of pure compassion, are as close to God as is a Christian, and consequently know Him equally well, although their knowledge is expressed in other words, or remains unspoken. For 'God is

Love'. And if He rewards those who seek after Him, He also gives light to those who approach Him, especially if they earnestly desire the light.

14

St. John says: 'Whosoever believes Jesus to be the Christ is born of God.' Thus whoever believes that, even if he assents to nothing else of what is affirmed by the Church, possesses the true faith. Hence St. Thomas is completely mistaken. Furthermore the Church, by adding to the Trinity, the Incarnation and the Redemption other articles of faith, has gone against the New Testament. To keep in line with St. John, it should never have excommunicated any except the Docetae, those who deny the Incarnation. The definition of faith according to the catechism of the Council of Trent (firm belief in everything taught by the Church) is very far removed from that of St. John, for whom faith was purely and simply belief in the Incarnation of the Son of God in the person of Jesus.

Everything has proceeded as though in the course of time no longer Jesus, but the Church, had come to be regarded as being God incarnate on this earth. The metaphor of the 'mystical Body' serves as a bridge between the two conceptions. But there is a slight difference, which is that Christ was perfect, whereas the Church is sullied by a host of crimes.

The Thomist conception of faith implies a 'totalitarianism' as stifling as that of Hitler, if not more so. For if the mind gives its complete adherence, not only to what the Church has recognized as being strictly necessary to faith, but furthermore to whatever it shall at any time recognize as being such, the intelligence has perforce to be gagged and reduced to carrying out servile tasks.

The metaphor of the 'veil' or the 'reflection' applied by the mystics to faith enables them to escape from this suffocating atmosphere. They accept the Church's teaching, not as the truth, but as something behind which the truth is to be found.

This is very far from faith as defined by the catechism of the Council of Trent. Everything proceeds as though, under the same name of Christianity and within the same social organism, there were two separate religions—that of the mystics and the other one.

I believe the former to be the true one, and that the confusion between the two has brought at the same time great advantages and great disadvantages.

According to the words of St. John, the Church

has never had the right to excommunicate any one who truly believed Christ to be the Son of God come down to earth in the flesh.

St. Paul's definition is broader still: 'belief that God exists and rewards those who seek after Him'. Neither has this conception anything in common with those of St. Thomas and the Council of Trent. There exists even a contradiction. For how could any one presume to contend that amongst heretics there has never been a single one who sought after God?

15

The Samaritans were in relation to the ancient Law what heretics are in relation to the Church. The 'perfect ones' among the Cathari (to take one example) were in relation to a host of theologians what the Good Samaritan of the parable is in relation to the priest and the Levite. In that case, what are we to think of those who allowed them to be massacred and gave their blessing to Simon de Montfort?

The Church ought to have learned from this parable never to excommunicate any one who practises the love of his neighbour.

There is not, as far as I can see, any real difference—save in the forms of expression—between the Manichaean and Christian conceptions concerning the relationship between good and evil.

The Manichaean tradition is one of those in which you may be quite certain of finding some truth if you study it with sufficient piety and attention.

Since Noah is a 'representation of Christ' (see Origen), a just man and a perfect, whose sacrifice was pleasing to God and saved humanity, and through the medium of whom God entered into a covenant with all men, his drunkenness and nakedness have probably to be understood in the mystical sense. In that case, the Hebrews must have distorted history, as Semites and murderers of the Canaanites. Ham must have shared in Noah's revelation; Shem and Japheth must have refused to share in it.

A Gnostic quoted by Clement of Alexandria (*Strom.*, VI, 6) affirms that the allegorical theology of Pherecydes (Pythagoras's master) is borrowed from the 'prophecies of Ham'—Pherecydes was a Syrian. He wrote: 'Zeus, as he was in the act of creating, transformed himself into Love....' Could it be that this 'Ham' was the son of Noah?

What makes one inclined to think so is the genealogical table. The descendants of Ham were the Egyptians, the Philistines (that is to say, the Aegeo-Cretans or Pelasgi in all probability), the Phoenicians, the Sumerians, the Canaanites—in other words, the whole of Mediterranean civilization immediately prior to historical times.

Herodotus, confirmed by numerous indications, declares that the Hellenes borrowed all their metaphysical and religious knowledge from Egypt by way of the Phoenicians and the Pelasgi.

We know that the Babylonians derived their traditions from the Sumerians—to whom must consequently be traced back the 'Chaldean wisdom'.

(Similarly, Druidism in Gaul was very probably of Iberian and not Celtic origin; for according to Diogenes Laërtius certain of the Greeks saw in it one of the origins of Greek philosophy, which otherwise would be incompatible with the late arrival of the Celts in Gaul.)

Ezekiel, in a magnificent passage in which he

compares Egypt to the tree of life and Tyre to the cherubim guarding it, confirms absolutely what Herodotus tells us.

It seems, therefore that the peoples descended from Ham, and in the first place the Egyptians, knew the true religion, the religion of love, in which God is a sacrificial victim as well as being an all-powerful ruler. Among the peoples descended from Shem and Japheth, some—like the Babylonians, the Celts, the Hellenes—received this revelation from the peoples descended from Ham after having conquered and invaded them. Others—the Romans, the Hebrews—rejected it out of pride and desire for national power. (Among the Hebrews, exceptions must be made in the case of Daniel, Isaiah, the author of the Book of Job and a few others; among the Romans, in that of Marcus Aurelius, and to a certain extent in that of men like Plautus and Lucretius.)

Christ was born in a land belonging to these two rebellious peoples. But the inspiration which lies at the heart of the Christian religion is twin-sister to that of the Pelasgi, Egypt and Ham.

Nevertheless, Israel and Rome set their mark on Christianity; Israel by causing the Old Testament to be accepted by it as a sacred book, Rome by turning it into the official religion of the Roman

Empire, which was something like what Hitler dreams* of doing.

This double—and well nigh original—defilement explains all the subsequent defilements that make the history of the Church such an atrocious one across the centuries.

Such a horrible thing as the crucifixion of Christ could only happen in a place in which evil very far outweighed good. But not only that, the Church, born and bred in such a place, must needs be impure from the beginning and remain so.

19

The Church is only perfectly pure under one aspect; when considered as guardian of the sacraments. What is perfect is not the Church; it is the body and blood of Christ upon the altars.

20

It does not seem that the Church can be infallible; for, in fact, it is continually evolving. In the Middle Ages, the saying 'Outside the Church there is no salvation' was taken in the literal sense by the doctrinal authorities of the Church. At any rate, the documentary records seem clearly to indicate this.

* Written in 1942

Nowadays it is understood in the sense of the invisible Church.

A council has declared anathema whoever does not believe that in Christ's saying ' . . . whoever is not born of water and the Spirit . . .' the word 'water' actually referred to the material element of baptism. On this count, all priests nowadays are anathemas. For if a man who has neither received nor desired to receive baptism can be saved, as is generally admitted at the present time, he must have been reborn of water and the Spirit in a certain sense, necessarily a symbolical one; consequently the word 'water' is taken in a symbolical sense.

A council has declared anathema whoever professes to be certain of final perseverance without having had a particular revelation. St. Theresa of Lisieux, shortly before her death, declared she was certain of her salvation, without adducing any revelation in support of this statement. That did not prevent her from being canonized.

If one asks several different priests whether such-and-such a thing is strictly an article of faith, one obtains different, and often dubitative, answers. That creates an impossible situation, when the edifice itself is so rigid that St. Thomas was able to put forward the affirmation referred to earlier.

There is something in all this which does not seem to fit.

21

In particular, the belief that a man can be saved outside the visible Church requires that all the elements of faith should be pondered afresh, under pain of complete incoherence. For the entire edifice is built around the contrary affirmation, which scarcely anybody today would venture to support.

No one has yet wanted to recognize the need for such a revision. One gets out of the difficulty by having recourse to miserable expedients. The cracks are plastered over with *ersatz* cement, shocking mistakes in logic.

Unless the Church recognizes this need soon, it is to be feared that it will not be able to accomplish its mission.

There is no salvation without a 'new birth', without an inward illumination, without the presence of Christ and of the Holy Spirit in the soul. If, therefore, salvation is possible outside the Church, individual or collective revelations are also possible outside Christianity. In that case, true faith constitutes a very different form of adhesion from that which consists in believing such-and-such an opinion. The whole notion of faith then needs to be thought out anew.

22

In practice, mystics belonging to nearly all the religious traditions coincide to the extent that they can hardly be distinguished. They represent the truth of each of these traditions.

The contemplation practised in India, Greece, China, etc., is just as supernatural as that of the Christian mystics. More particularly, there exists a very close affinity between Plato and, for example, St. John of the Cross. Also between the Hindu Upanishads and St. John of the Cross. Taoism too is very close to Christian mysticism.

The Orphic and Pythagorean mysteries were authentic mystical traditions. Likewise the Eleusinian.

23

There is no reason whatever to suppose that after so atrocious a crime as the murder of a perfect being humanity must needs have become better; and, in fact, taken in the mass, it does not appear to have done so.

The Redemption is situated on another plane—an eternal plane.

Speaking generally, there is no reason to establish any connection between the degree of perfection and chronological sequence.

Christianity was responsible for bringing this notion of progress, previously unknown, into the world; and this notion, become the bane of the modern world, has de-Christianized it. We must abandon the notion.

We must get rid of our superstition of chronology in order to find Eternity.

24

The dogmas of the faith are not things to be affirmed. They are things to be regarded from a certain distance, with attention, respect and love. They are like the bronze serpent whose virtue is such that whoever looks upon it shall live. This attentive and loving gaze, by a shock on the rebound, causes a source of light to flash in the soul which illuminates all aspects of human life on this earth. Dogmas lose this virtue as soon as they are affirmed.

The propositions 'Jesus Christ is God' or 'The consecrated bread and wine are the body and blood of Christ', enunciated as facts, have strictly speaking no meaning whatever.

The value of these propositions is totally different from the truth contained in the correct enunciation of a fact (for example: Salazar is head of the Portuguese Government) or of a geometrical theorem.

This value does not strictly speaking belong to the order of truth, but to a higher order; for it is a value impossible for the intelligence to grasp, except indirectly, through the effects produced. And truth, in the strict sense, belongs to the domain of the intelligence.

25

Miracles are not proofs concerning the faith (proposition anathematized by I cannot remember which council).

If miracles constitute proofs, they prove too much. For all religions have—and have always had—their miracles, including the strangest sects. Reference is made to dead persons having returned to life in Lucian. Hindu traditions are full of such stories, and it is said that even today, in India, miracles are regarded as events of no particular importance because of their banality.

To affirm either that the Christian miracles are the only authentic ones and all the others are untrue, or that they alone are brought about by God and all the others by the devil—that is a miserable expedient. For it is an arbitrary affirmation, and therefore the miracles prove nothing; they themselves need proving, since they receive from the outside the stamp of authenticity.

The same may be said with regard to prophecies and martyrs.

When Christ invokes his 'Καλὰ ἔργα', there is no reason for translating these by miracles. They can just as well be translated by 'good works', 'beautiful actions'.

Christ's attitude on this subject, as far as I understand it, was that he ought to be recognized as holy because he was perpetually and exclusively performing good.

He said: 'Without my works, they had been without sin'; but also, and putting the two things on the same level: 'Without my words, they had been without sin.' Now, his words were in no sense miraculous, only beautiful.

The very notion of the miracle is a Western and modern one; it is linked up with the scientific conception of the world, with which it is, nevertheless, incompatible. In what we regard as miracles, the Hindus see the natural effects of exceptional powers that are found in connection with few people, and more often than not in connection with saints. They thus constitute a presumption of saintliness.

The word 'signs' [or 'wonders'] in the Gospel does not mean anything more. It cannot mean anything more. For Christ said: 'Many will say to me: Have we not in thy name done many wonderful works? And I will say unto them: Depart from me, ye that work iniquity. . . .' And again: 'For there shall arise false Christs and false prophets, and shall show great signs and wonders; insomuch that, if it were possible, they shall deceive the very elect.' In Revelation (xiii. 3–4), the death and resurrection of Antichrist seems to be indicated.

In Deuteronomy it says: 'If a prophet comes speaking in the name of other gods, even if he perform miracles, he shall be put to death.'

If the Jews were wrong to put Christ to death, it was, therefore, not on account of his miracles, but on account of the holiness of his life and the beauty of his words.

As far as concerns the historical authenticity of the acts known as miracles, there are not sufficent motives for either affirming or denying it categorically.

If this authenticity is admitted, there are several possible ways of conceiving the nature of such acts.

There is one which is compatible with the scientific conception of the world. For that reason it is to be preferred. The scientific conception of the world, if properly understood, must not be divorced from true faith. God has created this universe as a network of second causes; it would seem to be impious to suppose there to be holes in this network, as though God were unable to attain his ends save by tampering with his own creative act.

If the existence of such holes is admitted, it becomes a scandal that God should not contrive some in order to save the innocent from affliction. It is only possible for resignation to arise in the soul at the affliction of the innocent through the contemplation and the acceptance of necessity, which is the inflexible concatenation of second causes. Otherwise, one is forced to have recourse to expedients which all end up by denying the very fact of the affliction of the innocent, and consequently by falsifying all understanding of the human condition and the core itself of the Christian conception.

Facts termed miraculous are compatible with the scientific conception of the world if one admits as a postulate that a sufficiently advanced form of science would be able to account for them.

This postulate does not do away with the link between such acts and the supernatural.

A fact can be linked with the supernatural in three ways.

Certain facts can be the results either of what takes place in the flesh, or of the action of the devil upon the soul, or of action on the part of God. Thus one man weeps with physical pain; another by the side of him weeps for thinking about God with a pure love. In both cases there are tears. These tears are the results produced by a psycho-physical mechanism. But in one of the two cases a wheel of this mechanism is a supernatural one; it is charity. In this sense, although tears are such an ordinary phenomenon, the tears of a saint in a state of genuine contemplation are supernatural.

In this sense, and in this sense alone, the miracles of a saint are supernatural. They are so on the same principle as that governing all material effects of charity. A gift of alms out of pure charity is as great a marvel as walking upon the waters.

A saint who walks upon the waters is in every respect analogous to a saint who weeps. In either case there is a psycho-physiological mechanism one of the wheels of which is charity—there lies the miracle, that charity can be a wheel in such a mechanism—and which produces a visible result. In the one case the visible result is the walking upon the waters, and in the other case the tears. The former is more uncommon—that is the only difference.

Are there certain facts which flesh alone can never produce, but only mechanisms in which either the wheel of supernatural love or else that of demoniacal hatred enters into play? Is walking upon the waters one of these?

That is possible. We are too ignorant to be able either to affirm or deny with regard to this matter.

Are there certain facts which neither the flesh nor demoniacal hatred can produce, which can only be produced by mechanisms having among their wheels charity? Such facts would constitute unimpeachable criteria of sainthood.

Perhaps there are some. There again our ignorance is too great for us to be able either to affirm or deny. But for this very reason, if such facts do exist, they cannot be of any use to us. We cannot make use of them as criteria, since we cannot be in any way certain with regard to them. That which is uncertain is unable to render another thing certain.

The Middle Ages were obsessed by the search for some material criterion of sainthood. There lies the significance of the search for the philosopher's stone. The quest of the Grail seems to bear on the same subject.

The true philosopher's stone, the true Grail, is the Eucharist. Christ has shown us what we are to think of miracles by placing at the very heart of the Church an invisible and in some sort purely conventional miracle (only the convention has been ratified by God).

God wishes to remain hidden. 'Thy Father which is in secret.'

Hitler could die and return to life again fifty times, but I should still not look upon him as the Son of God. And if the Gospel omitted all mention of Christ's resurrection, faith would be easier for me. The Cross by itself suffices me.

For me, the proof, the really miraculous thing, is the perfect beauty of the accounts of the Passion, together with certain glowing words of Isaiah's: 'He was oppressed, and he was afflicted, yet he opened not his mouth . . .', and of St. Paul's: 'Who, being in the form of God, thought it not robbery to be equal with God; but made himself of no reputation . . . and became obedient unto death, even the death of the cross. . . . He was made accursed.' That is what compels me to believe.

Indifference with regard to the miracles would not trouble me, were it not for the anathema pronounced by some council or other, since the Cross produces the same effect upon me as the resurrection does upon other people.

On the other hand, if the Church does not work out a satisfactory doctrine concerning so-called miraculous facts, a good many souls will be lost through its fault because of the apparent incompatibility between religion and science. And a good many others will be lost because, believing that God enters into the network of second causes in order to produce particular results with a particular intention, they impute to him the responsibility for all the atrocious happenings in which He does not intervene.

The current conception in regard to miracles either prevents the unconditional acceptance of God's will, or else compels one to turn a blind eye on the amount and nature of the evil existing in the world—an easy enough thing to do, evidently, from the depths of a cloister; or even in the world from within a restricted circle.

In fact, one notices a deplorable puerility in the case of a great many pious and even saintly souls. The Book of Job might never have been written, judging from the ignorance displayed about our human condition. For souls of this type, there are only sinners on the one hand, and on the other martyrs who die with a song on their lips. Which is why the Christian faith does not 'catch on', does not spread from soul to soul like a prairie fire.

Besides, if miracles possessed the nature, significance and value attributed to them, their rarity today (in spite of Lourdes and the rest) could induce the belief that the Church no longer had any part in God. For the resurrected Christ said: 'He that believeth and is baptized shall be saved; but he that believeth not shall be damned. And these signs shall follow them that believe. In my name shall they cast out devils; they shall speak with new tongues; they shall take up serpents, and if they drink any deadly thing, it shall not hurt them; they shall lay hands on the sick and they shall recover.'

How many believers are there at the present time, according to this criterion?

(Happily, this text is perhaps not authentic. But it figures in the Vulgate.)

26

The mysteries of the faith are not a proper object for the intelligence considered as a faculty permitting affirmation or denial. They are not of the order of truth, but above it. The only part of the human soul which is capable of any real contact with them is the faculty of supernatural love. It alone, therefore, is capable of an adherence in regard to them.

The role of the remaining faculties of the soul, beginning with the intelligence, is only to recognize that the things with which supernatural love is in contact are realities; that these realities are superior to their particular objects; and to become silent as soon as supernatural love actually awakens in the soul.

The virtue of charity is the exercise of the faculty of supernatural love. The virtue of faith is the subordination of all the soul's faculties to the faculty of supernatural love. The virtue of hope is an orientation of the soul towards a transformation after which it will be wholly and exclusively love.

In order that they may subordinate themselves to the faculty of love, the other faculties must each find therein their own particular good; and particularly the intelligence, which is the most precious of all after love. It is, indeed, effectively so.

When the intelligence, having become silent in order to let love invade the whole soul, begins once more to exercise itself, it finds it contains more light than before, a greater aptitude for grasping objects, truths that are proper to it.

Better still, I believe that these silences constitute

an education for it which cannot possibly have any other equivalent and enable it to grasp truths which otherwise would for ever remain hidden from it.

There are truths which are within its reach, within its grasp, but which it is only able to seize after having passed in silence through the midst of the unintelligible.

Is not this what St. John of the Cross means when he calls faith a night?

The intelligence is only able to recognize by experience, in retrospect, the advantages of this subordination to love. It does not divine them in advance. It has not to start with any plausible reason for accepting this subordination. And, indeed, this subordination is a supernatural thing, brought about by God alone.

The initial silence, lasting barely a moment, which pervades the entire soul in the interests of supernatural love, is the seed sown by the Sower; it is the grain of mustard-seed, practically invisible, that will one day become the Tree of the Cross.

In the same way, when one gives one's whole attention to a wholly beautiful piece of music (and the same applies to architecture, painting, etc.), the intelligence finds therein nothing to affirm or deny. But all the soul's faculties, including the intelligence, become silent and are wrapped up in listening. The listening itself is applied to an incomprehensible object, but one which contains a part of reality and of good. And the intelligence, which cannot seize hold of any truth therein, finds therein nevertheless a food.

I believe that the mystery of the beautiful in nature and in the arts (but only in art of the very first order, perfect or nearly so) is a sensible reflection of the mystery of faith.

27

We owe the definitions with which the Church has thought it right to surround the mysteries of the faith, and more particularly its condemnations (. . . *anathema sit*) a permanent and unconditional attitude of respectful attention, but not an adherence.

We likewise owe a respectful attention to opinions that have been condemned, to the extent —be it ever so small—to which their content, or the life of those who propounded them, contains some show of good.

Intellectual adherence is never owed to anything whatsoever. For it is never in any degree a voluntary thing. Attention alone is voluntary. And it *alone* forms the subject of an obligation.

If one tries to bring about in oneself an intellectual adherence by the exercise of the will, what actually results is not an intellectual adherence, but suggestion. That is what Pascal's method amounts to. Nothing degrades faith more. And there necessarily appears, sooner or later, a compensatory phenomenon in the shape of doubts and 'temptations against faith'.

Nothing has contributed more towards weakening faith and encouraging unbelief than the mistaken conception of an obligation on the part of the intelligence. All obligations other than the one of attention which itself is imposed on the intelligence in the exercise of its function stifle the soul—the whole soul, and not the intelligence only.

28

The jurisdiction of the Church in matters of faith is good in so far as it imposes on the intelligence a certain discipline of the attention; also in so far as it prevents it from entering the domain of the Mysteries, which is foreign to it, and from straying about therein.

It is altogether bad in so far as it prevents the intelligence, in the investigation of truths which are the latter's proper concern, from making a completely free use of the light diffused in the soul by loving contemplation. Complete liberty within its own sphere is essential to the intelligence. The intelligence must either exercise itself with complete liberty, or else keep silent. Within the sphere of the intelligence, the Church has no right of jurisdiction whatsoever; consequently, and more particularly, all 'definitions' where it is a question of *proofs* are unlawful ones.

In so far as 'God exists' is an intellectual proposition—but *only* to that extent—it can be denied without committing any sin at all either against charity or against faith. (And, indeed, such a negation, formulated on a provisional basis, is a necessary stage in philosophical investigation.)

Christianity has, in fact, since the very beginning, or nearly so, suffered from an intellectual malaise. This malaise is due to the way in which the Church has conceived its power of jurisdiction and especially the use of the formula *anathema sit*. Wherever there is an intellectual malaise, we find the individual is oppressed by the social factor, which tends to become totalitarian. In the thirteenth century, especially, the Church set up a beginning of totalitarianism. For this reason it is not without a certain responsibility for the events of the present day. The totalitarian parties have been formed as a result of a mechanism analogous to the use of the formula *anathema sit*.

This formula and the use to which it has been put prevent the Church from being Catholic other than in name.

29

Before the advent of Christianity, an indeterminate number of men, both in Israel and outside it, may *possibly* have gone as far as the Christian saints in the love and in the knowledge of God.

Similarly, since Christ's time, in the case of that portion of humanity outside the Catholic Church ('infidels', 'heretics', 'unbelievers'). And in a more general way, it is doubtful whether since Christ's time there have been more love and knowledge of God in Christendom than in certain non-Christian countries, such as India.

30

It is very *probable* that the eternal destiny of two children that have died within a few days after birth, one of them having been baptized and the other not, is identical (even if the parents of the second child had no intention at all of having it baptized).

31

Among all the books of the Old Testament, only a small number (Isaiah, Job, the Song of Solomon, Daniel, Tobias, part of Ezekiel, part of the Psalms, part of the Books of Wisdom, the beginning of Genesis ...) are able to be assimilated by a Christian soul, together with a few principles scattered here and there throughout the others. The rest is indigestible, because it is lacking in an essential truth which lies at the heart of Christianity and which the Greeks understood perfectly well— namely, the possibility of the innocent suffering affliction.

In the eyes of the Hebrews (at any rate before the exile, and save for exceptions) sin and affliction, virtue and prosperity go hand-in-hand, which turns Jehovah into an earthly not a heavenly Father, visible and not invisible. He is thus a false god. An act of pure charity is impossible with such a conception.

32

One might lay down as a postulate:

All conceptions of God which are incompatible with a movement of pure charity are false.

All other conceptions of Him, in varying degree, are true.

The love and the knowledge of God cannot really be separated, for as it says in Ecclesiastes: '*Praebuit sapientiam diligentibus se.*'

33

The story of the creation and of original sin in Genesis is true. But other stories about the creation and original sin in other traditions are also true and also contain incomparably precious truths.

They are different reflections of a unique truth untranslatable into human words. One can divine this truth through one of these reflections. One can divine it still better through several of them.

(Folklore especially, when properly interpreted, is found to contain a wealth of spirituality.)

34

The Church does not seem to have perfectly carried out its mission as the conserver of doctrine—very far from it. Not only because it has added what were perhaps abusive precisions, restrictions and interdictions; but also because it has almost certainly lost real treasures.

As evidence of this we have certain passages in the New Testament of marvellous beauty but which are nowadays absolutely incomprehensible, and which cannot always have been so.

To begin with, nearly the whole of the Apocalypse.

The passage in St. John: ' . . . he that came by water and blood, even Jesus Christ; not by water only, but by water and blood. . . . And there are three that bear witness in earth, the Spirit, and the water, and the blood: and these three agree in one'. The same St. John's insistence upon the water and blood that came out of Christ's side.

The talk with Nicodemus is also very mysterious.

St. Paul ' . . . be ye rooted and grounded in love, that ye may be able to comprehend with all saints *what is the length, and breadth, and height, and depth;* and to know the love of Christ, which passeth knowledge . . . .' Already Origen, separated from St. Paul by so short an interval of time, comments on this beautiful passage in the most banal way.

The passage in St. Paul concerning Melchisedec ' . . . without father, without mother, without descent . . . but made like unto the Son of God, abideth a priest continually'.

The doctrine of the resurrection of the flesh. The

living flesh which must perish, and the 'spiritual flesh' (*pneumatikê*—should we keep in mind the Pythagorean theory of the *pneuma* contained in the semen?) which is eternal. The relationship between this doctrine and the importance attached to chastity ('Every sin that a man doeth is without the body; but he that committeth fornication sinneth against his own body.' 'Meats for the belly, and the belly for meats: but God shall destroy both it and them. Now the body is not for fornication, but for the Lord, and the Lord for the body.') [What is here the meaning of the word 'body', so curiously placed in opposition to 'belly'?]

The study of Hindu doctrines casts a much more vivid light thereon than any Christian text that I know of. Christians have never said, so far as I am aware, *why* chastity (and more especially virginity) possesses a spiritual value. This is a serious lacuna, and one that keeps away a great many souls from Christ.

The relationship between the doctrine of the Redemption in which man is the end in view (and which, as Abelard very rightly observed, is quite unintelligible) and the apparently contrary doctrine suggested by the words 'God hath desired to give his Son many brethren'. (This would then mean that we had been created *because of* the Incarnation.)

The mysterious relationship between the Law and sin, expressed by St. Paul in sometimes so strange a fashion. Here again, Hindu thought furnishes a little light.

The insistence shown in repeating such expressions as ' . . . hanged on a tree', ' . . . made accursed'. Here, there is something irreparably lost.

The extraordinary violence shown by Christ towards the Pharisees, representatives of the spirit of Israel in its purest form. Hypocrisy, narrow-mindedness and corruption, vices common to every type of clergy owing to the weakness of human nature, do not sufficiently explain such violence. And certain words which have a mysterious sound suggest that there was something else: 'Ye have taken away the key of knowledge.'

The Pythagoreans named 'key' the mediation between God and creation. They also named it harmony.

The words 'Be ye perfect, even as your Father which is in heaven is perfect', coming immediately after the words 'Your Father which is in heaven, who maketh his sun to rise on the evil and on the good, and sendeth rain on the just and on the unjust' imply a whole doctrine which, as far as I know, is not developed anywhere. For Christ cites as the supreme characteristic of God's justice precisely what is always brought forward (example of Job) with the object of accusing Him of injustice, namely, that He favours the good and the wicked indifferently.

There must have been in Christ's teaching the notion of a certain virtue attaching to indifference, similar to that which may be found in Greek stoicism and Hindu thought.

These words of Christ remind one of the supreme cry uttered by Prometheus: 'Heaven by whom for all the common light revolves . . . '.

(Moreover, this light and this rain also possess probably a spiritual significance, that is to say, that all—both in Israel and outside it, both in the Church and outside it—have grace showered upon them *equally*, although the majority reject it.)

That is absolutely contrary to the current conception whereby God arbitrarily sends down more grace on one man, less on another man, like some capricious sovereign; and that on the pretext that He does not owe it to any man! He owes it to his own infinite goodness to give to every creature good in all its fulness. We ought rather to believe that He showers continually on each one the fulness of his grace, but that we consent to receive it to a greater or lesser extent. In purely spiritual matters, God grants all desires. Those that have less have asked for less.

The very fact that *Logos* has been translated by *verbum* shows that something has been lost, for λόγος means above all *relation*, and is a synonym for ἀριθμός, number, with Plato and the Pythagoreans. Relation, that is to say proportion. Proportion, that is to say harmony. Harmony, that is to say mediation. I would translate as follows: In the beginning was Mediation.

(All this opening part of the Gospel according to St. John is very obscure. The words 'He was the true Light, which lighteth every man that cometh into the world' contradicts absolutely the Catholic doctrine concerning baptism. For in that case, the Word secretly dwells in every man, whether he be baptized or not; it is not baptism which causes It to enter into the soul.)

A great many other passages could be cited.

On the one hand, the lack of understanding shown by a certain number of the disciples, even after the day of Pentecost (proved by the episode concerning Peter and Cornelius), on the other hand, the massacres brought about by persecution, explain this deficiency in the matter of transmission. Perhaps by the beginning of the second century A.D. all those who had understood had been killed, or nearly all.

The liturgy also contains words with a mysterious sound to them.

Quaerens me sedisti lassus must refer to something else besides the account of the episode concerning the woman of Samaria in St. John. By considering these words in relation to the theme of a great number of accounts in folklore, a vivid light is thrown upon the latter.

The idea of God going in quest of man is something unfathomably beautiful and profound. Decadence is shown as soon as it is replaced by the idea of man going in quest of God.

Beata (arbor) cujus brachiis—Pretium pependit saeculi—Statera facta corporis—Tulitque praedam Tartari.

This symbol of the balance is astonishingly profound. The balance played an important part in Egyptian thought. At the moment Christ died, the sun was in the constellation of the Ram and the moon in that of the Balance (Libra). Note that this sign used to be called the 'Pincers of Cancer'. Writers did not begin to give it the name 'Balance' until shortly before the Christian era (one month before, the sun had been in the Fish and the moon in Virgo; cf. the symbolical meaning attached to the Fish [I.X.Θ.U.Σ.]).

If one ponders this metaphor, Archimedes's words 'Give me a fulcrum and I will shake the world' may be regarded as a prophecy. The fulcrum is the Cross, point of intersection between time and eternity.

Sicut sidus radium—profert Virgo filium—pari forma.—Neque sidus radio—neque mater filio—fit corrupta. These verses have a very strange sound.

And the preceding strophe (*Sol occasum nesciens— stella semper rutilans—semper clara*) takes on an extraordinary meaning when considered in connection with a tale of the American Indians, according to which the Sun, in love with a chieftain's daughter who has disdained all suitors, descends to earth in the form of a sick youth, very nearly blind and miserably poor. A star accompanies him, disguised as a wretched old woman, the youth's grandmother. The chieftain puts his daughter's hand up for competition and lays down very severe tests. The miserable youth, though ill and lying on a pallet, contrary to every expectation, is alone successful in passing them all. The chieftain's daughter goes to his home as his bride, in spite of his repulsive appearance, out of fidelity to her father's word. The wretched young man is transformed into a wonderful prince and transforms his wife, changing her hair and apparel into gold.

One could not, however, attribute this tale to any Christian influence, it would seem . . .

In the liturgy for holy days, *ipse lignum tunc notavit, damna ligni ut solveret*— . . . *arbor una nobilis: nulla silva talem profert, fronde, flore, germine* have also a strange sound. These are magnificent words; they must have been related to a whole symbolism that is now lost. Moreover, the whole liturgy for Holy Week has as it were a startling flavour of antiquity about it.

The legend of the Grail suggests a nowadays unintelligible combination, doubtless brought about during the years which followed the death of Christ—although the poems date from the twelfth century—between Druidism and Christianity.

Note that the Church has never condemned the poems dealing with the Grail, in spite of the evident mixture between Christianity and a non-Christian tradition.

Almost immediately after the Passion, Herod was sent into enforced residence at Lyons, accompanied by a numerous suite in which there must have been some Christians. (Was Joseph of Arimathaea perhaps among them?) The Druids were exterminated by Claudius a few years later.

The *Dionysiacs* of Nonnos, a poem by an Egyptian (probably a Christian) of the sixth century, but which only concerns itself with Greek gods and astrology, and yet bears some very singular points of resemblance to the Apocalypse, must have been inspired by some similar sort of combination.

(*N.B.* It concerns a king, Lycurgus, already referred to in Homer, who has treacherously attacked Dionysus unarmed and forced him to take refuge *at the bottom of the Red Sea.* He was king of the Arabs living to the south of Mt. Carmel. Geographically, it can hardly be a question of anything other than Israel. If it were admitted that Israel was looked upon by the ancients as a people accursed because of having rejected the notion of the mediating, suffering and redemptive God revealed to Egypt, one would understand what is otherwise inexplicable: namely, that Herodotus, avid as he was of every curious detail of a religious nature, should never have mentioned Israel. Note that Israel was predestined to serve as Christ's birthplace—but also to have him put to death. Note also that there are numerous accounts testifying to the fact that Dionysus and Osiris are the same God. If we possessed the Egyptian version of the story of Moses, we should perhaps receive some surprises...)

The *Rune of Odin* referred to higher up, if it is not earlier than all contact with Christianity, would doubtless represent the remains of a similar blending. It would not be any less extraordinary.

Were there, perhaps, at the beginning, some of Christ's apostles who understood the words 'Go ye and teach all nations' in the way which I believe to be the correct one?

35

The understanding of Christianity is rendered almost impossible for us by the deep mystery surrounding the story of those early times.

This mystery bears first of all upon Christianity's relations on the one hand with Israel, and on the other hand with the religious traditions of the *gentes*.

It is extremely unlikely that there were not in the early stages attempts at a syncretism analogous to the one dreamed of by Nicholas of Cusa. Now, there is no trace of any condemnation pronounced by the Church against such attempts. (Nor, for that matter, was Nicholas of Cusa himself ever condemned.) And yet everything has happened, in fact, just as if they had been condemned.

Beside the silly nonsense talked by Clement of Alexandria—who was no longer even aware of the close bonds uniting Greek classical philosophy to the religion of the Mysteries—there must have been men who saw in the Glad Tidings the crowning touch to that religion. What became of their works?

Porphyry declared that Origen had symbolically interpreted the Hebrew Scriptures by making use of the secret books of the Pythagoreans and the Stoics. Yet when Origen talks about Greek philosophy, it is with the evident pretension of refuting it. Why? Because it happens to be the rival shop across the way? Or is it for some other reason? Was he trying to conceal his debt towards it? And if so, why?

This passage from Porphyry clearly shows that the Mysteries were entirely made up of allegories.

Eusebius quotes this passage, and calls Porphyry a liar for having said that Origen began by 'hellenizing'. But he does not deny the rest.

Eusebius also quotes the most curious letter from Bishop Melito to Marcus Aurelius, written in a very friendly tone (*Hist*. IV, 26): 'Our philosophy was first developed among the barbarians, but came into full bloom among thy peoples (τοῖς δοῖς ἔθνεδιν) during the great reign of Augustus.'

These 'barbarians' can only be the Hebrews. But what does the rest of the sentence signify?

Augustus died in A.D. 14. Christ was then a boy. Christianity did not exist.

'Our philosophy'—might that mean our *Logos*,

the Christ? Did it have its flowering (that is, its youthful expansion) among the *gentes* in Greece or Italy?

The bishop adds: 'The best proof that our *Logos* developed contemporaneously with the fine beginnings of the Empire in the interests of good, is that it suffered no vexation under the rule of Augustus, but, on the contrary, attained to all splendour and glory in accordance with the wishes of all.'

We always talk about the 'hidden life in Nazareth'. Only we forget that, though it is indeed true that this life was a hidden one, strictly speaking we do not know whether it unfolded itself in Nazareth at all.

This is all we know through the Gospel about the life of Christ before he was baptized by John.

He was born in Bethlehem. When still quite a small child, his family took him down to Egypt. He remained there for an unknown period. (Joseph returned after the death of Herod, but there is nothing to show that this was immediately afterwards; some years may have elapsed.) When twelve years old he spent the Easter festival in Jerusalem. His parents were then settled in Nazareth. (It is curious that St. Luke does not mention the flight into Egypt.) At the age of thirty he was baptized by John. And that is strictly all.

This is again a very singular mystery.

A third mystery is that of the relations between Christianity and the Empire. Tiberius wanted to have Christ placed in the Pantheon and refused first of all to persecute the Christians. Later on his attitude changed. Piso, Galba's adopted son, probably belonged to a Christian family (cf. works of M. Hermann). How are we to explain the fact that men like Trajan and above all Marcus Aurelius should have so relentlessly persecuted the Christians? Yet Dante places Trajan in paradise. . . . On the other hand Commodus and other villainous emperors rather favoured them. And in what circumstances did the Empire later on come to adopt Christianity as the official religion? And on what conditions? What degradation was the latter made to suffer by way of exchange? In what circumstances was accomplished that collusion between the Church of Christ and the Beast? For the Beast of the Apocalypse is almost certainly the Empire.

The Roman Empire was a totalitarian and grossly materialistic regime, founded upon the exclusive worship of the State, like Nazism. A thirst for spirituality was latent amongst the wretched ones subjected to this regime. The Emperors realized from the very beginning how necessary it was to assuage it with some false mysticism, for fear that a true mysticism should arise and upset everything.

An attempt was made to transfer the Eleusinian Mysteries to Rome. These mysteries had almost certainly—convincing indications point to this— lost all genuine spiritual content. The atrocious massacres which had so frequently taken place in Greece and especially in Athens since the Roman conquest, and even before, had very likely caused their transmission to be interrupted; the Mysteries were perhaps re-manufactured by initiates of the first degree. This would explain the scorn with which Clement of Alexandria talks about them, although he may at one time have been an initiate himself. However, the attempted transfer failed.

To make up for this, the Druids and the fol- lowers of the secret cult of Dionysus were exter- minated, the Pythagoreans and all the philosophers pitilessly persecuted, the Egyptian cults prohibited, the Christians treated as we know.

The pullulation of oriental cults in Rome at that time resembles exactly that of sects of a theoso- phical order at the present day. As far as one is able to make out, then as now, they were not the genuine article, but artificial creations designed for snobs.

The Antonines represent something like an oasis in the appalling history of the Roman Empire. How is it that they were able to persecute the Christians?

One may ask oneself whether under cover of the enforced underground existence genuinely criminal elements had not insinuated themselves among the Christians.

Above all it is necessary to bear in mind the apocalyptic spirit which inspired them. The expectation of the imminent coming of the Kingdom exalted them and gave them courage to perform the most extraordinary acts of heroism, just as the imminent expectation of the Revolution does nowadays in the case of the Communists. There must be many points of resemblance between these two psychologies.

But, in both cases, such expectancy also constitutes a very great social danger.

The historians of antiquity are full of stories about cities where, as a result of certain slaves having been granted their freedom by some tyrant for one reason or another, it became impossible for masters to make themselves obeyed by those that remained.

Slavery was such an unnatural state that it was only bearable for those whose souls were

crushed by the total absence of hope. As soon
as a ray of hope appeared, disobedience became
rife.

What an effect must have been produced by the
hope contained in the Glad Tidings! The Glad
Tidings meant not only the Redemption; they
meant even more the practically certain fact of the
very imminent coming on earth of Christ in all his
Glory.

In St. Paul, for every recommendation to be
kind and just addressed to the masters, there are
perhaps ten recommendations addressed to the
slaves, enjoining them to work and be obedient.
This might, if necessary, be explained by the remains of social prejudices left in him in spite of
Christianity. But it is far more likely that it was
much easier to persuade Christian masters to show
kindness than it was to persuade Christian slaves,
intoxicated by the expectation of the Last Day, to
show obedience.

Marcus Aurelius perhaps disapproved of slavery;
for it is not true that Greek philosophy, with the
exception of Aristotle, acted as the apologist of that
institution. According to Aristotle himself, certain
philosophers condemned it as being 'absolutely contrary to nature and reason'. Plato, in the *Statesman*,
only conceives of it being legitimately employed

in dealing with criminals, in the same way as we do in the matter of imprisonment and forced labour. But Marcus Aurelius had as his business that of keeping order above all other things. He would remind himself bitterly of the fact.

Catholics readily justify the massacres of heretics by citing the social dangers inherent in heresy. It never occurs to them that the persecutions of the Christians in the early centuries are open to the same justification, with at least as great a show of reason. Much greater no doubt, for no heresy contained an idea so profoundly disturbing as the practically certain right to expect the imminent coming of Christ the King.

It is certain that a wave of disobedience among the slaves of the Empire would have brought the whole edifice toppling down in the midst of frightful disorders.

By the time of Constantine, the state of apocalyptic expectation must have worn rather thin. Besides, the massacres of Christians, by hindering the transmission of the most profound doctrine, had perhaps—and even probably—emptied Christianity of a great part of its spiritual content.

Constantine was able to carry out successfully in the case of Christianity the operation Claudius had been unsuccessful in carrying out in the case of Eleusis.

But it was neither in the interests nor in keeping with the dignity of the Empire that its official religion should appear as the continuation and crowning point of the centuries-old traditions of countries conquered, crushed and degraded by Rome—Egypt, Greece and Gaul. In the case of Israel, that did not matter; in the first place the new law was very far removed from the old law; and then, above all, Jerusalem no longer existed any more. Besides, the spirit of the old law, so widely separated from all mysticism, was not so very different from the Roman spirit itself. Rome could come to terms with the God of Hosts.

Even the Jewish national spirit, by preventing a great many Christians, from the start, from recognizing the affinity between Christianity and the authentic spirituality of the *gentes*, was for Rome a favourable element in Christianity. This spirit, strangely enough, had even communicated itself to converted 'pagans'.

Rome, like every colonizing country, had morally and spiritually uprooted the conquered countries. Such is always the effect of a colonial conquest. It was not a question of giving them back

83

their roots. It was necessary they should be still a little bit further uprooted.

[Note, as confirmation of this, that the only pagan prophecy which has ever been mentioned by the Church is that of the Sibyl, which the Roman tradition had annexed. (Furthermore, the fourth eclogue clearly shows that there really was a messianic expectation in Rome, very similar to the one in Judaea and equally in the flesh.)]

Christianity, subjected to the combined influence of Israel and Rome, succeeded brilliantly in this task. Even today, wherever it is carried by missionaries, it exercises the same uprooting effect.

All this is a mass of suppositions, of course.

But there is one thing which is a practical certainty, namely, that people have wanted to hide something from us, and they have succeeded in doing so. It is not by chance that so many texts have been destroyed, that so much obscurity surrounds so essential a party of history.

There has probably been a systematic destruction of documents.

Plato managed to escape it; by what lucky stroke of fortune? But we do not possess the *Prometheus unbound* of Aeschylus, which must have allowed a glimpse of the true significance of the story of Prometheus, the love uniting Prometheus to Zeus, already touched upon, but no more, in the *Prome-theus enchained*. And how many more treasures lost!

The historians have come down to us with great gaps. Nothing has been left of the Gnostics, and little enough of the Christian writings of the early centuries. If there were any in which Israel's privileged position was not recognized, they have been suppressed.

Yet the Church has never declared that the Judaeo-Christian tradition was alone in possessing revealed Scriptures, sacraments, and supernatural knowledge about God. It has never declared that there was no affinity at all between Christianity and the mystical traditions of countries other than Israel. Why? Might it not be because the Holy Spirit has in spite of everything saved it from telling a lie?

These problems are today of *capital, urgent and practical importance*. For since all the profane life of our countries is directly derived from 'pagan' civilizations, as long as the illusion subsists of a break between so-called paganism and Christianity, the latter will not be incarnate, will not impregnate the whole of profane life as it ought to do, will remain separated from it and consequently non-active.

How our life would be changed if we could see that Greek geometry and the Christian faith have sprung from the same source!

FOR THE BEST IN PAPERBACKS, LOOK FOR THE

In every corner of the world, on every subject under the sun, Penguin represents quality and variety—the very best in publishing today.

For complete information about books available from Penguin—including Penguin Classics, Penguin Compass, and Puffins—and how to order them, write to us at the appropriate address below. Please note that for copyright reasons the selection of books varies from country to country.

In the United States: Please write to *Penguin Putnam Inc., P.O. Box 12289 Dept. B, Newark, New Jersey 07101-5289* or call 1-800-788-6262.

In the United Kingdom: Please write to *Dept. EP, Penguin Books Ltd, Bath Road, Harmondsworth, West Drayton, Middlesex UB7 0DA.*

In Canada: Please write to *Penguin Books Canada Ltd, 10 Alcorn Avenue, Suite 300, Toronto, Ontario M4V 3B2.*

In Australia: Please write to *Penguin Books Australia Ltd, P.O. Box 257, Ringwood, Victoria 3134.*

In New Zealand: Please write to *Penguin Books (NZ) Ltd, Private Bag 102902, North Shore Mail Centre, Auckland 10.*

In India: Please write to *Penguin Books India Pvt Ltd, 11 Panchsheel Shopping Centre, Panchsheel Park, New Delhi 110 017.*

In the Netherlands: Please write to *Penguin Books Netherlands bv, Postbus 3507, NL-1001 AH Amsterdam.*

In Germany: Please write to *Penguin Books Deutschland GmbH, Metzlerstrasse 26, 60594 Frankfurt am Main.*

In Spain: Please write to *Penguin Books S. A., Bravo Murillo 19, 1° B, 28015 Madrid.*

In Italy: Please write to *Penguin Italia s.r.l., Via Benedetto Croce 2, 20094 Corsico, Milano.*

In France: Please write to *Penguin France, Le Carré Wilson, 62 rue Benjamin Baillaud, 31500 Toulouse.*

In Japan: Please write to *Penguin Books Japan Ltd, Kaneko Building, 2-3-25 Koraku, Bunkyo-Ku, Tokyo 112.*

In South Africa: Please write to *Penguin Books South Africa (Pty) Ltd, Private Bag X14, Parkview, 2122 Johannesburg.*